THE DRIVERS HANDBOOK

Arthur E. Hanvold

AuthorHouse™
1663 Liberty Drive, Suite 200
Bloomington, IN 47403
www.authorhouse.com
Phone: 1-800-839-8640

© *2007 Arthur E. Hanvold. All rights reserved.*

No part of this book may be reproduced, stored in a retrieval system, or transmitted by any means without the written permission of the author.

First published by AuthorHouse 9/12/2007

ISBN: 978-1-4343-0262-5 (sc)

Library of Congress Control Number: 2007902294

Printed in the United States of America
Bloomington, Indiana

This book is printed on acid-free paper.

INTRODUCTION

On behalf of ……………………………..…………
I.……………………………………………...………
Assign this book to…………………………..……..
Date……………………………………….…………..

This book will assist you in the awareness of:

Some policies, procedures and safe acts,
attitude, sportsmanship, and being a team player
while sharing our highways.
The importance of Due Diligence and
some of the responsibilities as a
True Professional Driver.

I, Art Hanvold dedicate this book to you and your
well being as a True Outstanding Individual
changing the image of Our Industry
to be more positive.

Remember – You are responsible for
your own actions.

This book consists of
guidelines, suggestions and
information to assist you in becoming a

"TRUE PROFESSIONAL DRIVER"

BOOK ONE

This book is written for you the driver.
The purpose of this book is to help you become
more knowledgeable in the Transportation Industry.
Lord only knows – there's a lot to remember,
for us that can't remember it all –
There is a lot of good advice.

BOOK TWO

Will be coming out in the near future.
We would like to hear from you.
Please send your comments about this book,
or any advice you may have and
would like to see in the next book.
Thank you
You can contact us at the address below:

Email: bunart@telus.net

© 2007 Arthur E. Hanvold All rights reserved
No part of this book may be reproduced, stored in a
retrieval system, or transmitted by any means
without the permission of the author.

Cover: Brenden Hanvold

THE SUCCESSFUL DRIVER OF TODAY AND TOMORROW WILL DISPLAY THESE QUALITIES!

Be a team player

Be punctual

Neat and clean appearance

Good communicator

High degree of accountability

Respect high level of confidentiality

High level of reading, writing and math skills

Have a positive attitude

Be prepared for on going training
to upgrade your skills

Good mechanical aptitude

Willing to comply with company policy

To abide by all the Rules & Regulations

Table of Contents

Introduction v
Book One vi
Book Two vi
The Successful Driver vii

Accountability 1
A Personal Mission Statement 1
Attitude 2
Air Brakes 3
In House Air Brake Inspection 4
Brake Adjustment And Some Procedures 5
BRAKES AND DUE DILIGENCE 5
Attention 4 Wheelers 6
Attitude 7
Anger 7
Anger Management 7
Ask The Questions 9
Assume 9

Backing A Tractor-trailer 10

Circle Check 12
Confidence 14
Commitment To Be A Responsible Driver 14
Cutting In Front Of Vehicles 15

Due Diligence 17
Driver Trainer 19
Driver Attitude 20
Discipline Yourself 21
Driver's Prayer 22
Driving Habits 23
Effective Habits 23

Exercise 24
Breathing Exercise 24
Emergency Situations 24
Expect The Unexpected 26
US Emergency Phone Numbers 27
US Emergency Cell Phone Numbers Hazardous Spill 29
Canada Emergency Phone Numbers 31
Ergonomics Hazards 33
Explanation Of Log Book Violations 34

For The New Or Young Driver 35
The Job On Hand 36
Fifth Wheel Securement 37
Frozen Brakes 37
Fuel Conditioner 38
Fire Extinguishers 39
Fatality Figures – Canada 40
Family Discipline 41
The 4-Way Test 42
Freedom To Choose 42

Give Yourself, Family, Friends 43

Healthy Eating Habits 44
Habits For A Healthy Relationship 45
Secret For A Happy Marriage 45
Honesty And Friendship 46
How Do We Learn Or Teach 46
Hats Off To The Lady Trucker 47
How To Deal With Stress 49
Hours Of Service 50
Hours Of Service – U.S.A 50
Hours Of Service – Canada 51

Important Messages 52
Idling Time And Fuel Costs 53

Jokes 54

Load Securement	57
Some Load Securement Problems	57
Lights	59
Law Enforcement	60
Meeting	61
Meal Allowance	61
Money	61
Metric Conversion Tips	62
Normal Commercial Driver	63
Notes	64
Personal Principles	65
Proper Attitudes And Skills	66
Persistence	67
Personality Traits	67
Buiilding And Maintaining A Good Work Relationship	69
Patience Is A Virtue	70
Praise For Drivers	70
Paperwork	71
Phonetic Alphbet	73
Placarding	74
Professional Driver's Opinion	76
Protecting Yourself From Identity Theft	78
Question: Asked To Drivers	82
Road Rage	85
The Right To Refuse	85
Smile	86
Some Driving Distractions	88
A "Seeing Expert"	88
Six Secrets Of High Energy People	89
Safe Work Practices	89
Safety Tip	90
Slow Vehicles	90

Speeding Hurry Up Driver 90
Some Safe Work Practices And Ideas 91
Safety Tip – Think Before You Lift 91
Safety Gear 92
Safe Work Hazards 92
Spill Cleanup Suggested Procedures 94
Speeeding And The Aggressive Driver 95
Substance Abuse Policy 96
Six Positions Of The Two Vehicle Accident 97

Some Statistics On Fatal Collisions 98
Self Assessment Quiz 99

The Absentee Parent 100
The Lady Behind The Man Behind The Wheel 101
Truck Ride 101
Ten Differences Between A Winner And A Loser 102
Treat People The Way They Need To Be Treated 104
The Trucker And The Tourist 106
Ten Tips For Safe Fuel - Efficient Driving 107
T.d.g. Or Hazmat 108
Ten Common Driving Mistakes 109
The Real Cost Of An Accident 110

Use Of Safety Equipment 111
UTA The Used Truck Association 112

Weight Loss Tip 116
What Is Wisdom ? 118
Windshields 119
Winter Survival Gear 119
Work Alone 120
Watch Those Diesel Prices 120
You Have What It Takes 121

ACCOUNTABILITY

It's all about life and you.
This is a story about people named Anybody,
Somebody, Nobody, and Everybody.

There is an important job to be done and
Everybody was sure that Somebody would do it.
Anybody could have done it, but Nobody did it.
Somebody got angry about that, because
it was Everybody's job.
Everybody thought Anybody could do it,
but Nobody realized that Everybody
would not do it.
It ended up that Everybody blamed Somebody,
when Nobody did what Anybody
could have done.

You are accountable for the consequences of
your actions, or the lack of your actions.
Remember: The first impression –
may be your last.

A PERSONAL MISSION STATEMENT

Succeed at home #1
Never compromise with honesty
Remember other people involved
Hear both sides before judging
Obtain counsel of other (committee)
Defend those who are absent

Maintain a positive attitude
Keep a sense of humor
Be neat in appearance and work
Don't fear mistakes
(be cautious and sincere)
Listen twice as much as you speak
Concentrate all abilities and efforts
into the safety of oneself and others.

ATTITUDE

Accept that some days you're the pigeon and some days you're the statue.
Always keep your words soft and sweet,
just in case you have to eat them.
Never let anyone change your attitude.
One example of this:
You are driving down the highway and someone gives you the bird and cuts you off.
If that changes your attitude – you just let the other person become the winner.
So don't let anything or anybody change
your attitude. Drive professional,
be kind and considerate
to the users of the highways.
Remember that you are the only professional driver out there today.
Others are just learning or new to the area.
If you drive with that attitude, you will
be less likely to be involved in a mishap.
Show your real professionalism

A fellow told me that birthdays are good for you, the more you have, the longer you live.
You may be the only person in the world, but you may also be the world to one person.
So look after yourself. – **Be Happy**
A happy person is one who can enjoy the scenery on a detour. There is no use complaining about the detour, as you
cannot change it anyway.
So enjoy the drive

AIR BRAKES

There is a few Air Brake courses and exams that are clear and easy to understand. These will improve your knowledge of the operation of the air brake system, that has been very vague in our industry.
We could all use a refresher on this and it would eliminate the fines, out of service criteria related to air brakes out of adjustment , not to mention the safety of yourself and the other people using the highways. I understand that some Insurance companies have a course available to its members. So check with your insurance company and see if they do.
Remember – there is a lot to learn in our industry
so any refreshers you can take, are an improvement
to safety and to yourself.

IN HOUSE AIR BRAKE INSPECTION

A Tractor / Trailer Combination – A Good rule of Thumb
Bring air pressure up to maximum (120 psi)
Shut engine down. Allow system to stabilize with wheels chocked and system fully charge for 1 minute. After 1 minute check pressure gauges for 2 minutes. Pressure drop should not exceed 2 psi per service reservoir on the tractor plus 2 psi per trailer added on.
Next step – Give full brake application to 100 psi
Hold for 1 minute to allow system to stabilize.
After 1 minute, check gauges for air loss for another 2 minutes.
Air loss in the tractor and trailer, during these 2 minutes, should not exceed 4 psi
For the tractor and 2 psi for each trailer per service reservoir.
Pump air down to ensure that warning buzzer and lights work.
They should activate no less than 60 psi.
Next step – Keep pumping brakes. Emergency tractor and trailer valves should pop at not less than 20 psi. Start engine: Air pressure from 50 psi to 90 psi should not take more than 3 minutes.
This indicates air compressor is ok.
Spring brake check – Start tractor in low gear, just get it moving, put in clutch, pop tractor protection valve. You should get a snap stop. This indicates that the spring brakes are in proper working order.
The same application applies for the trailer.
Maxi spring brake – When maxi brakes are on check and make sure all push rods are extended,
if not, they are broken and need replaced.

BRAKE ADJUSTMENT AND SOME PROCEDURES

One thing we have found that makes brake adjustments and brake inspections a lot easier is; put plastic tie straps on push rods with brakes released, and as close to the brake pot as possible. That will be your indicator rather than chocking them.

Then apply brakes and measure. Another procedure that I do rather than chock wheels is apply trailer brakes, do the tractor adjustment, then apply the tractor brakes, for adjustment.
If automatic slack adjusters are out of adjustment, try some hard brake applications 80 – 100 pounds. This application is what sets up automatic slack adjusters. If this procedure fails to adjust the brakes, and you have to adjust them manually, report this to your dispatch office or shop – as they need to be replaced.

BRAKES AND DUE DILIGENCE

It is our duty as drivers to know and understand the importance of brake operation and adjustments. We know that this must be performed at all times, and that we comply with all the rules in our industry.

If you decide to leave on a trip without checking your equipment, or brakes – and they are not properly adjusted, and you are involved in an incident
YOU BECOME LIABLE.
Which is called DUE DILIGENCE
two words that mean so much.
It is also very important that you and your equipment meet the national safety code.

An example of Due Diligence:

You say that your equipment is all ok and down the road you are involved in an incident, and you and your equipment don't meet the national safety code – you become anywhere from 10 – 100% liable for that incident.

ATTENTION 4 WHEELERS

For what it's worth:
In our travels over many years, I have talked to many people and tow truck drivers.
I have been told that 80-90% of all vehicles in accidents and being towed, from missing corners or sliding off roads are 4 wheelers, as they don't slow down enough for road conditions.
4 wheel drive doesn't hold you on the road in icy weather conditions.

ATTITUDE

Attitudes count more than achievements.
Forget yourself long enough to lend a helping hand. Great
opportunities often disguise themselves in small tasks.
The little things in life determine the big things.
Your abilities are the natural
talents you are born with.
An example is:
Some people have a way with words.
Some people have a way with expressions.
Some people show their emotions.

ANGER

Why you must control anger
It is only one letter short of danger.

A person with a proper attitude
turns negatives into positives.

Remember: Life is a Learning Experience
Accept the task at hand.

ANGER MANAGEMENT

Knowing how to handle and respond to anger
is very crucial to your well being.
Do not keep your anger bottled up inside, do you

yell and scream at your partner, kids or family?
Do you drive too fast and reckless on highways?
What people do with their anger and how they
handle it affects other people around them.
Everyone of us gets angry at one time or another,
that's natural. It's how we handle anger that counts.
Whether it's at someone else or oneself.
For all our own short comings some of the causes of
anger are stress, fear, annoyance, frustration,
resentment and disappointment.

Anger can be a healthy motivator if used right.
If not, it can become an overwhelming destructive
force that you may do something wrong and that
you could be sorry for the rest of your life.
That's why it is so important that you control your
anger and know the importance of managing it.

Turn an anger into a positive rather than a negative.
Have a sense of humour.
Try to find a healthy constructive attitude
when dealing with situations that arise.
Don't make any hasty decisions without first
giving it some thought. If someone can change
your positive attitude – then you have played into
his hand. He wins – You lose.
Remember you are a better person
when you are positive.
Learn to turn negatives into positives.
The secret is – answer with a question.

ASK THE QUESTIONS

If you don't know or understand something
Ask the Question.
If the person you asked the question – laughs
at you ask him again. He probably doesn't know
the answer, and says what a foolish question
Remember: There is not a foolish question.
So ask someone else the same question –
many times you know the answer when the
person starts to answer the question, this is
when you realize that you do know the answer,
and they have reinforced your thoughts.
It is better to be sure, than not ask the question
then wonder if you are right.
Remember: Life is a learning experience.

ASSUME

Don't assume that someone has
done this or that to your unit.
Example:
The shop mechanic installs new brakes on the
unit, you fail to check for proper adjustment
and you are involved in an incident,
when the brakes are out of adjustment
YOU become liable because you assumed
that the mechanic had adjusted the brakes.
The bottom line is –
DON'T ASSUME ANYTHING

BACKING A TRACTOR-TRAILER

1. When backing a tractor-trailer, turn the steering wheel in the opposite direction to where you want the trailer to go. You can also place your hand on the bottom of the steering wheel and move your hand in the same direction as you want the trailer to go. The truck-tractor must follow an S-shape in order to bring the trailer around smoothly.

2. Always back the vehicle slowly and use both rear view mirrors. Never forget that there is a blind spot directly behind the trailer that is not visible in the mirrors.

3. Avoid unnecessary backing by planning ahead.

4. Sound the horn as a safety precaution before backing. Repeat for every length backed.

5. If possible, ask someone to act as a guide. The guide must be able to see the path the vehicle is taking. The driver must be able to see the guide. Stop if you cannot see the guide.

6. Even though you have a guide, the driver is still responsible for all movements of the vehicle.

7. If you don't have a guide available, always check the area where you are backing before

beginning the move. Get out of your vehicle, walk behind it and visually check the area. look for obstructions and clearance.

8. If the backing distance exceeds two vehicle lengths, stop, get out and visually recheck the areas behind, above, below and around the entire unit.

9. Keep your foot off the throttle. You will rarely need to use it to start your unit backing. Always use the lowest gear available. Move very slowly and keep your right foot covering the brake pedal in case you need to stop quickly.

Straight line backing is the easiest and the safest form of backing. Most times you will have a clear view in both mirrors of the space that you are backing into.

Backing from the blind side is harder to see where you are going. Once the backing has started you will mostly be using the right side mirror including the convex mirror. You should stop and get out of the truck often to check your position. This type of backing is the most difficult and also potentially the most dangerous.

Avoid it if you can.

CIRCLE CHECK

AROUND THE VEHICLE
1. Check vehicle for unrepaired damage to lights, clearance clusters, bumper and mud flaps.
2. Check all tires for inflation and missing valve caps. Check wheel lugs and nuts.
3. Check spring for sag and U-bolts for tightness.
4. Check rear view mirror mountings, operation of doors, door handles and latches.
5. Check fuel tanks and fuel level, air vent and properly locking cap.
6. Check tarps, lashings, tailgates and rear doors.

IN THE ENGINE COMPARTMENT
1. Check radiator for leaks, coolant level and properly locking cap.
2. Check fan for bent blades, loose mountings and belt tension.
3. Check oil level.
4. Check battery for electrolyte level, cracks, and corrosion.
5. Check air cleaner for proper attachments.
6 Check quickly for proper for obvious breaks or loose connections in electrical systems, coolant hoses and vacuum hoses.

WITH ENGINE STARTED
1. Check engine for ease of starting and smooth operation.

2. Check operation of hand throttle, choke, and accelerator pedal.
3. Check brakes of air or vacuum operated types.
4. Check operation of all instrumental panel gauges.
5. Check operation of windshield wipers.
6. Check for unusual noise in clutch and transmission, when pedal is depressed then release, with engine running and the transmission is in neutral.

FIFTH WHEEL
1. Check fifth wheel mounting.
2. Check operation and position of fifth wheel locking handle.
3. Check locking brake to make sure it is engaged.
4. Check lower coupler plate for proper connection and condition.
5. Check brake hoses for proper connection and condition.
6. Check light cables for connection and condition.

IN THE CAB
1. Check feel and lash of brake.
2. Check hand brake for travel and locking.
3. Check horn -windshield wipers – fuel gauge
4. Check rear view mirrors and all lights by getting in and out of the cab.

CONFIDENCE

One of the greatest obstacles in life is
confidence in ones self.
That is the major reason for
not being successful or happy in life.
Sometimes we get in a hurry up lifestyle
Don't let this happen to you.
There's an old saying which is so true to life.
The hurrier I go …..The behinder I get.
You need time for yourself,
family, friends, and your job.
Some of us get into a comfort zone
and won't venture beyond that comfort zone.
Even if we get a gut feeling or that inner voice telling us:
"We can do Better"
Fear of being a failure holds us back, so trust your feelings and
venture out to become a better person.
If you want change –
Plot a course of action and execute it.
Your only time limit is your self doubt.
Be positive and take all the classes and courses,
to help you better yourself.

COMMITMENT TO
BE A RESPONSIBLE DRIVER

Plan your route
Maintain your vehicle
Minimize your distractions

Focus your attention
Know your surroundings
Share your space
Watch your speed
Keep your distance
Signal your intention
Always wear your seatbelt

Remember – Safe driving is your responsibility whether to or from work, or as a professional driver.
Drive like a True Professional

CUTTING IN FRONT OF VEHICLES

There are many reasons why this is dangerous.

Never cut in front of another vehicle, or get in between two trucks without adequate space.
That is putting you in a death zone.

If the truck had to stop fast and there is not enough space between the two trucks, or enough stopping distance for the rear truck. By your cutting in between the two trucks, you are using up some of
his stopping distance.

Never cut in front of a truck especially when coming off a merge exit. So many drivers are intimidated by the big rig and aren't sure what to do so they come to a stop in front of him. That

truck could be weighing in excess of 50 tons and
need the length of a football field to stop. The same
goes for coming off a side road onto a main
highway, this has caused so many accidents
that could have been prevented.

Always use the 1001 – 1002 counting method for
allowing space, if you don't allow enough space
you are asking for trouble.

I know it's hard to leave enough space between you and the vehicle
ahead, as someone is always cutting
in front of you, taking up your space. Most often
the person cutting you off or cutting directly in front of you is
because he is being tailgated by a speeding
vehicle and he feels pressured to get out of the way.
but the best advice is to stay in that lane and not get
caught in between two trucks.

Most accidents are caused by bullish speeding
drivers that only care about themselves If they
would only slow down a few notches, our highways
would become a safer place to drive.

The news media should be blaming the careless
driver when weather and road conditions are bad,
rather than the road and weather.

A good driver drives according to the road and
weather conditions. The good driver will get off the road and wait
for better conditions.

DUE DILIGENCE

It is extremely important that you know and fully understand your
responsibilities, the well being of your company and fellow
employees depend on it.
The main concern is your safety –
and the safety of others.
Be a true team player – and abide by all the rules and regulations
of our industry

TWO WORDS – **DUE DILIGENCE**
- MEAN SO MUCH
Are you doing your part on Due Diligence?
Are you doing a proper Pre and Post trip?
Are you doing your best to avoid a bad situation?
You are in the driver's seat.
You have a moral and legal obligation
to take all reasonable precautions to ensure
safe operation of your vehicle.

It's called "Due Diligence"
And it's in the best interest of
you and your Company
So be a true Professional.

DUE DILIGENCE

It's a huge network.
Try to learn and understand Due Diligence

1. If you don't know, say so, don't fudge it as this could create a problem.
2. Get proper training.
3. Set a good example for others.
4. Make sure you fully understand the process of due diligence.

A FEW THOUGHTS AND IDEAS THAT MAY HELP YOU

1. Enforce safety and due diligence.
2. Be accountable for your actions.
3. Set a good example for others.
4. Keep your log book in order, and don't go over in hours.
5. Keep clean and tidy.
6. Wear PPE equipment when required.
7. Report any accidents, incidents, or near misses.
8. Watch out for other drivers.
9. Take responsibility for your own actions.
10. Go to training classes – these are documented and filed.
11. Erase all the due diligence on your behalf when possible, keep you and your equipment above the National Safety Code.
12. Drive according to the rules and regulations of our highways. Remember your equipment is like a loaded gun if not driven properly.
13. The fines are high for unsafe equipment.

DRIVER TRAINER

Driver trainer – policy procedures reminder.
It is your responsibility to ensure that the trainee
is getting a fair chance and you as a trainer are
providing that opportunity.
These are some of the qualifications that
you must have in order to be a good
Instructor and Trainer.
To hold this position you must be.
kind, considerate, and a caring person.
Remember the day you first started.
A good trainer is always positive.
Be a good listener.
Is capable of turning negatives into positives.
Any trainee under your supervision
must be treated fair and given a considerate
and equal opportunity to succeed.
You the trainer – play a very important role
In our Safety Department Program.
You must ensure the importance of Safety Orientation and On The
Job Training.
Teach Job – Hazards and Responsibilities.
Workers right to refuse unsafe work conditions.
Company enforcement policies.
Handle incidents and questions in
a business like manner.

Remember **"Due Diligence"**

DRIVER ATTITUDE

I believe there are a lot of drivers out there that don't know or don't care what they are doing.

They are not safety conscious nor do they care about the other people that they are sharing the highways with. They drive very bullish and ignorant – It's sure not like it used to be.

It's a shame that a lot of drivers are out there for themselves, but it doesn't have to be that way.

If all drivers would slow down to the posted speeds and be a little more considerate, what a difference it would make.

A few examples:

No speeding – This costs you many of dollars.

The faster you drive, the faster you replace the fuel consumed.

Wear and tear on your tractor plus tire wear.

Pay the price for speeding. When paying $2.15 per gallon speed is not cheap. Try driving at different speeds and record your savings.

I know that people have changed their way of operating and have profited $10,000 to $20,000 in a year, in fuel costs alone – not to mention wear and tear on their vehicles and themselves.

When you are speeding, this brings fatigue on oneself, not to mention road rage and aggressive driving.

**SLOW DOWN – BE SAFE
AND ENJOY THE SCENERY
If we all drive professionally – We can change the image of the truck driver.**

DISCIPLINE YOURSELF
TO BE A BETTER PERSON

With today's shortage of good drivers, a lot of companies turn their head on good honest discipline. Also some rules are not enforced. Good honest discipline will eliminate most infractions and moods.
By abiding by all the rules and regulations in our industry, not letting some other person change your attitude, an example:
If you let the other person change your attitude, he becomes the "Winner and you the "Loser".

So why would let someone you don't even know, change your attitude?
You become the winner. Even though at times it's hard – (to keep smiling".

Remember your truck is like a weapon,
if not driven professionally.
Don't get involved in road rage, tailgating,
speeding to mention a few of the DON'TS
in our industry.

Drive accordingly to weather
and road conditions.

Remember highway speeds are posted
for ideal conditions.

DRIVER'S PRAYER

Lord Jesus – please make our travels safe
Grant me a steady hand and watchful eye
I pray that no act of mine will mar or
take away the gift of life in any way.
Using my knowledge and experience,
guide me and all others safely
down our highways.
May I never miss the beauty of our world
by speeding and aggressive driving.
I pledge to drive with loving concern of
others to my every destination.
I pray that you will help others to understand the
importance of sharing our roads and highways,
before it's too late and a fatality has happened.
Lord I am trusting in you and your sending of
Guardian Angels to watch over us
as we're making our journeys.
Amen

So driver, before putting your vehicle in gear,
You may want to say a prayer, asking
for God's guidance and your well being.

I do believe in the power of prayer, and
I thank God for giving me life,
and this opportunity to share.

DRIVING HABITS

You and your family are driving down the road. Have you given any thought about your driving aggressively, speeding, tailgating, horn honking, swerving in and out of traffic?
Your children are in the back seat, from day one they are learning your driving habits, good or bad without you even realizing it.
So drive according to the weather, rules and regulations. You don't have to drive a big rig in order to be a professional driver.
Remember: You are a teacher also as you are traveling with children. If you need to discipline children, pull over to a safe place and stop.

I know a lady that was traveling down the highway, she reached back to discipline the children and drove into the ditch.
This could have been a roll over with some very serious results.

EFFECTIVE HABITS
Knowledge – What to – Why to
Skills – How to
Desire – Want to

EXERCISE

Those who think they have not the time
for body exercise – Will sooner or later
find time for body illness.

Here are a few ways for some exercise
Park a block or two away
from where you are going.
Take stairs instead of elevators.

BREATHING EXERCISE

Breathe deep through the nose and hold,
Exhale through the mouth.

EMERGENCY SITUATIONS

In emergency situations avoid panic,
improvise and weigh the risks.
Read and carry an emergency handbook,
as there is a lot to remember.
If someone is choking and can't get air, or make noise, you will need to do the Heimlich maneuver, get help on the way, you or someone will need to call 911, EMS or the operator for assistance.
These instructions are for persons one year
of age or older, who are choking.

1. Do not interfere with a person who is choking, as long as he can cough forcefully, encourage him to cough. It may be all that is needed to dislodge the blocking.

2. If this fails and the victim is coughing or breathing with extreme difficulty, or he can no longer cough or breathe, quickly ask him if he is choking. If he is unable to speak or nods his head "yes" have someone call for medical aid and begin the Heimlich maneuver. (Immediate intervention is in order, too if the victim clutches his throat – an instinctive sign of choking or turns blue.)

3. Stand behind him and, with your arms around him, clench your fist and thrust it, thumb knuckle inward, at a spot well below the breastbone, slightly above the navel, and well away from either side of the rib cage.

4. Hold your fist with the other hand and pull both hands towards you with a quick upward and inward thrust from the elbows.

   You are trying to elevate the diaphragm so the air thus forced out of the lungs may dislodge the blockage. Repeat continuously until the blockage is dislodged or the victim becomes unconscious.

EXPECT THE UNEXPECTED

Every driver that has been in an accident, figured this could not happen to him or her, that this always happens to someone else, NOT ME.
Drive every road like it was the first time. Avoid tailgating and speeding.
Example: I've heard guys say "I've been over that road so many times I could drive it with my eyes closed "- You don't know what's around that next corner, no matter how many times you have driven that road.

SO EXPECT THE UNEXPECTED

If you travel the roads and highways that way,
you are likely to be in an incident.
Another example:

You traveled this road many times before, just before a sharp corner, when shifting down, then you don't have any rpms to make the downshift. Next he put on the brakes, he had a bad air leak in the foot valve(in the computer box directly below the foot valve) a fire erupted which was
the major cause of the roll over.

US EMERGENCY PHONE NUMBERS

STATE	POLICE PH	EMERGENCY PH
Alabama	334-242-4371 gen	911
Alabama	334-242-4395 mcs	911
Alaska	907-428-7200	911
Arizona	602-223-2000	911
Arkansas	501-619-8000	911
California	916-657-7261	911
Colorado	303-239-4500	911
Connecticut	860-685-8000	911
Delaware	302-739-5901	911
D.C.	202-737-4404	911
Florida	850-487-3139	911
Georgia	404-657-9300	911
Idaho	208-846-7512	208-772-8585
Illinois	217-786-7103	911
Indiana	800-582-8440	911
Indiana	317-899-8577	911
Iowa	515-281-5824	800-525-5555
Kansas	785-296-6800	911
Kentucky	502-695-6300	800-222-5555
Kentucky	502-695-6380	
Louisiana	225-925-6006	911
Maine	207-624-7000	911
Maryland	410-486-3101	911
Massachusetts	617-740-7600	911
Michigan	617-332-2521	911
Minnesota	651-282-6871	911
Mississippi	601-987-1530	911
Missouri	573-751-3313	800-525-5555

US EMERGENCY PHONE NUMBERS

STATE	POLICE PH	EMERGENCY PH
Montana	406-444-3780	911
Nebraska	402-471-4680	911
Nevada	775-687-5300	911
New Hampshire	603-271-2575	800-852-3411
New Hampshire	603-271-3636	
New Jersey	609-882-2000	911
New Mexico	505-827-9300	911
New York	518-436-2825	911
North Carolina	919-733-7952	911
North Dakota	701-328-2455	800-472-2121
Ohio	614-466-2660	877-772-8765
Oklahoma	405-425-2424	911
Oregon	503-378-3720	911
Oregon	503-378-3735	911
Pennsylvania	717-783-5599	911
Rhode Island	401-444-1000	911
South Carolina	903-896-7920	911
South Dakota	605-773-3105	911
Tennessee	615-251-5175	911
Texas	512-414-2000	800-525-5555
Utah	801-965-4379	911
Vermont	802-244-8775	911
Virginia	804-674-2000	804-553-3444
Washington	360-753-6540	911
West Virginia	304-746-2100	911
Wisconsin	608-266-3212	911
Wyoming	307-777-4305	911

US EMERGENCY CELL PHONE NUMBERS
HAZARDOUS SPILL
REPORTING NUMBERS

STATE	EMERGENCY CELL PHONE	HAZARDOUS SPILL REPORT PHONE
Alabama	*47 or 911	800-843-0699
Alaska	911	907-269-3063
Arizona	911	602-390-7894
Arkansas	911	800-322-4012
California	911	916-845-8911
Colorado	303/329/4501/911	877-518-5608
Connecticut	911	860-424-3338
Delaware	911	800-662-8802
D.C.	911	none
Florida	911	850-413-9911
Georgia	911	800-241-4113
Idaho	*47	800-632-8000
Illinois	911	800-782-7860
Indiana	911	888-233-7745
Indiana	911	515-281-8694
Iowa	*55 or 911	none
Kansas	*47	913-281-0991
Kentucky	800-222-5555	800-928-2380
Louisiana	911	225-342-1234
Maine	911	800-482-0777
Maryland	911	866-833-4686
Massachusetts	911	888-304-1133
Michigan	911	800-292-4706
Minnesota	911	800-422-0798

STATE	EMERGENCY CELL PHONE	HAZARDOUS SPILL REPORT PHONE
Mississippi	911	800-222-6362
Missouri	*55	573-634-2436
Montana	911	406-444-0379
Nebraska	911	402-471-2186
New Hampshire	911	800-346-4009
New Jersey	911	877-927-6337
New Mexico	911	505-827-9329
New York	911	800-424-8802
North Carolina	911	800-858-0368
North Dakota	*2121	800-472-2121
Ohio	877-772-8765	800-282-9378
Oklahoma	911	800-522-0206
Oregon	911	800-248-6782
Pennsylvania	911	800-541-2050
Rhode Island	911	888-372-7341
South Carolina	911	888-481-0125
South Dakota	911	605-773-3296
Tennessee	911	800-262-3300
Texas	800-525-5555	800-832-8224
Utah	911	801-536-4123
Vermont	911	800-641-5005
Virginia	804-553-3444	800-468-8892
Washington	911	800-258-5990
West Virginia	911	800-642-3074
Wisconsin	911	800-943-0003
Wyoming	911	307-777-7781

CANADA EMERGENCY PHONE NUMBERS AND HAZARDOUS SPILL REPORTING PHONE NUMBERS

PROVINCE	POLICE/ EMERGENCY	HAZARDOUS SPILL REPORT #
Alberta	911	800-222-6514
British Columbia	911	800-663-3456
Manitoba	911	204-981-7111
New Brunswick	911	800-565-1633
Newfoundland	911	800-563-2444
Nova Scotia	911	800-565-1633
Northwest Territories		867-920-8130
Nunavut		867-975-5925
Ontario	911	800-268-6060
Prince Edward Island	911	800-565-1633
Quebec	911	866-694-5454
Saskatchewan	911	800-667-7525
Yukon Territory (Whitehorse area only)	911	604-666-0370

"If the area is not serviced by 911 Dial 0 and ask the operator for assistance"
NOTE: These numbers may have changed or have been updated.

NOTES

ERGONOMICS HAZARDS

Physical disorders and stress that can cause harm to the human body, resulting from poor posture.

Improper handling of material and / or equipment, improper seating support, fatigue, monotony and improper work / rest cycles are considered ergonomics hazards

Examples:

Poor lighting

Improper seating

Doing the same thing for
a long period of time

Not getting the time to
get outside for fresh air

And a short walk

Working through break periods

EXPLANATION OF
LOG BOOK VIOLATIONS

1. Log missing
2. Date missing/Duplicate Logs
3. Miles driven missing
4. Name of carrier missing
5. Vehicle numbers missing
6. Driver's signature missing
7. Co-driver name missing
8. Company terminal address missing
9. Hours missing
10. Ten hour violation
11. Shipping document missing
12. Over maximum average MPH
13. Stop/start locations not the same
14. 15 hour violation
15. From & To missing
16. Violations of 60/70 hour rule
17. Trip lease incorrect
18. Log falsification
19. Tire check improperly noted
20. Graph incorrect
21. No driving time for miles driven
22. Different logs for the same day
23. Changes in duty status missing – use abbreviations for names of city.

If your log book is properly completed and up to date, you will eliminate a fine.

FOR THE NEW OR YOUNG DRIVER
A FEW DO'S AND DON'TS

When first starting out be a good listener.

Don't speed, stay under the speed limit at least 10mph.

Get the feel of things, like taking corners and hauling top heavy loads.

Get experience on wet and icy roads.

Drive careful in windy road conditions.

Be aware of heavy traffic and lane changing.

By driving slower, you can concentrate on making the right moves, rather than speeding and not having the control.

Don't let dispatch push you into breaking the rules, this will only cost you in the end.

Drive according to the rules and regulations of our industry – they are for your well being and safety.

Remember to be a true professional. One who never thinks he knows it all, and is willing to acknowledge change, learn, and help his fellow trucker and the people sharing the highways.

THE JOB ON HAND

When doing a job safely, with concern
About one self and the safety of others
That's called private and public victory.

The Five Seeing Habits

Aim High In Steering:
Look as far down the road as possible to uncover important information to make appropriate decisions.

Get the Big Picture:
Maintain the proper following distance so you can comfortably determine the true hazards around your vehicle. Don't tailgate others.

Keep Your Eyes Moving:
Scan – Don't stare. Constantly shift your eyes while driving. Active eyes keep up with changing
traffic conditions.

Leave Yourself an Out:
Be prepared. Surround your vehicle with space in front and at least on one side to escape conflict.

Make Sure They See You:
Communicate in traffic with your horn, lights and signals to establish eye contact with
motorists and pedestrians.

FIFTH WHEEL SECUREMENT

Some drivers were talking about fifth wheels coming unhooked from their trailers, and couldn't figure out how the trailer became unhooked as the fifth wheel was still closed.

Here's what happens:

When you're backing under a trailer, and the trailer is too high – the pin will ride on top of the jaws.

They will close, withstand a tug test, and everything seems ok. They will ride there for quite some time until driving into a twisting tilting turn. The wheel will then lift the trailer high enough to become disengaged. You can only determine this by looking underneath and from behind. How do I know this? - I've had it happen to me.

FROZEN BRAKES

Frozen brakes are costing companies and yourself many hours of down time. Sometimes in the thousands of dollars. Preventative maintenance would eliminate this problem.

A few examples are:
Draining air tanks, servicing air dryers however, if brakes won't release and you have to use alcohol, use only a couple of teaspoons in the red air line – Never use alcohol in the blue line.

Use only lubricated brake line anti-freeze,
or you will have major problems
with trailer valves.

**Some ABS Trailer Brakes need
100 plus pounds before they release.**

**Before using any alcohol or anti-freeze
In your brake system**

Consult your office.

FUEL CONDITIONER

**FUEL CONDITIONER WILL DISPLACE
OXYGEN WHEN IT IS SPILLED
IN A CONFINED AREA.**

**IT CAN CAUSE ASPHYXIATION
AND DEATH.**

It is a known fact that a driver had a bottle of fuel conditioner
spilled under his bunk.
A blood test at the doctors office
revealed that he had a lack of
oxygen in the blood.
The problem was traced back to
the spilled fuel conditioner.

FIRE EXTINGUISHERS

Good housekeeping is essential in the prevention of fires. Fires can start anywhere at any time. This is why it is important to always keep fire extinguishers visible and easy to get at. Fire extinguishers have to be properly maintained to do the job. When temperature is a factor, make sure to choose the right fire extinguisher.

TYPES OF FIRES

CLASS	TYPE OF FIRE	RECOMMENDED EXTINGUISHERS	FIGHT THE FIRE
A	Wood, paper, rags, rubbish and other combustible materials.	Water from hose pump type can pressure ext. and soda acid Extinguishers	Soak fire completely, even the smoking embers
B	Flammable liquids, oil and grease.	ABC units, dry chemical foam and carbon dioxide ext.	Start at the base of the fire and use a swinging motion left to right. Keep fire away from you.
C	Electrical Equipment	Carbon Dioxide and dry chemical (ABC units)	Use short bursts on the fire. When the electrical current is shut off on a class C fire, it can become Class A and ignite materials around it.

FATALITY FIGURES – CANADA
Approximately every 38 minutes
there is a fatality on our highways.

Fatality Figures – U.S.A.

Approximately every 12 minutes someone dies in a motor vehicle accident, every 10 seconds an injury occurs and every 5 seconds a crash occurs.
Many of these accidents occur commuting to and from work. Employers pay the price in a round about way. Employee shortage equals loss in production, not to mention the hardships this brings to your family. I feel that every company should have a drive safe program for all employees.
It's to their benefit as well as yours.
You may be one of those drivers that know it all, and figure you don't need help or knowledge. If that's the case then get involved in assisting in or on a committee - and help the program.
One fine example is the use of seatbelts, they have proven the reduction of injuries in accidents.
So wear yours.
The bottom line goes like this:
The person that died 12 minutes ago thought this would not happen to him, it always happens to someone else.
Be aware, drive defensively, learn when you can.
The # 1 killer is speed and aggressive driving.
Don't rush to your death –
Slow down and abide by the rules,
weather and road conditions.

FAMILY DISCIPLINE

Good honest discipline is love.
If you love your family – discipline them
Accordingly, along with yourself.
Remember: Life is a learning process
and we will never know it all.
If you think you know it all–
then you have a real problem.
Some feedback from kids:

1. They're always telling me to get off the computer. (Set a time frame)

2. My dad plays a lot on the computer. (Instead of playing with me)

3. My parents get mad when we forget to throw things in the trash or clean up after ourselves. (Don't get mad – use some honest discipline)

4. It bugs me when my parents send me to my room for doing something wrong. (Have them stand in the corner or sit on a chair.)

5. I wish my parents wouldn't make all my decisions. (Help me make a good decision)

6. When I take my stuff away from my brother or sister. (My parents may get mad- but they still love me.)

THE 4-WAY TEST

Of the things we think, say and do

1. Is it the TRUTH?

2. Is it FAIR to all concerned?

3. Will it build GOODWILL
   and BETTER FRIENDSHIPS?

4. Will it be BENEFICIAL to all concerned?

FREEDOM TO CHOOSE

Remember – we have the freedom to choose
and to make decisions
This day and age – you are held accountable
for your actions and decisions
The two words are - **Due Diligence**

If you are unsure of your answer or decision –
Ask the question or questions
If you don't know the answer –
(Say So – No person has all the answers)

**GIVE YOURSELF, FAMILY, FRIENDS
YOUR COMPANY AND
THE ENVIRONMENT
THE PLUS 6 TREATMENT**

1. **LOOK AHEAD AND DRIVE DEFENSIVELY**
   Be alert – Have foresight

2. **SHIFT PROGRESSIVELY**
   Easier on you, your equipment and the environment

1. **SHUT ENGINE OFF WHEN YOU CAN**
   Save fuel and the economy

2. **SLOW DOWN**
   Speeding gets you in trouble

5. **BE PHYSICAL AND MENTALLY FIT**
   Watch your eating habits and get exercise

6. **NEVER LET ANYONE CHANGE YOUR ATTITUDE**
   Be a defensive driver – Don't react negatively.

**ABANDON OLD HABITS
LEARN NEW TECHNIQUES
REMEMBER: YOU ARE THE ONLY
PROFESSIONAL ON THE ROAD TODAY**

HEALTHY EATING HABITS
**All those travelers out there combating driver
fatigue should eat a banana.**

They contain three natural sugars – sucrose, fructose, and glucose combined with fiber, a banana gives an instant, sustained boost of energy. Research has proven that two bananas provide enough energy for a 90 minute strenuous workout. It can also help overcome or prevent a substantial number of illnesses and conditions, making it
a must for our daily diet.
Bananas are extremely high in potassium so, the US Food and Drug administration has just allowed the banana industry to make official claims for the fruit's ability to reduce the risk of blood pressure and stroke.
High in fiber, including bananas in the diet, can help restore normal bowel action,
and eliminate laxatives.
Bananas have a natural antacid effect in the body, so if you suffer from heartburn, try eating a banana for relief. Bananas can also help people trying to give up smoking. The B6 and B12 they contain, as well as the potassium and magnesium in them, help the body from the effects of nicotine withdrawal. Eating bananas as a part of the regular diet can cut the risk of death by strokes as much as 40%. So a banana really is a natural remedy for many ills.

Bananas must be the reason monkeys are so happy !

HABITS FOR A HEALTHY RELATIONSHIP

1. Talk, talk, talk.
2. Have a date once in a while.
3. Fight fair.
4. Admit when you're wrong.
5. Let small things slide.
6. Hold hands.
7. Say Thank You
8. Make the effort.
9. Keep it surprising.
10. Kiss and make up.
11. Leave love notes.
12. Say I Love You.
13. Marry only when you are able to support a wife.
14. When you speak, look into their eyes.
15. Save when you're young – spend when old.
16. Don't go into debt – if there's a way out.
17. Good company and conversation is a virtue.
18. Your character can be damaged – only by you.
19. Retiring after the day – Did I do well?
20. Am I a good Samaritan?
21. How can I grow more positive?

SECRET FOR A HAPPY MARRIAGE

A friend of ours told us his secret for a successful marriage, that he made a deal with his wife. When they were first married, that she could make all the small decisions and he would make all the big decisions. After 53 years of marriage there were no big decisions.

HONESTY AND FRIENDSHIP
A TRUE STORY

Our daughter and her husband put their house up for
sale. Everyday for the first week to ten days, the
For Sale sign at the end of the street
was lying down.
One evening the doorbell rang – the little eight year
old neighbor girl and her mother were at the door.
The mother said "my daughter has something to tell
you" The little girl, crying at this point said "I'm
very sorry for taking your sign down everyday,
because I don't want yous to move away.
The mother then explained that she was unaware
of this until now, and the daughter couldn't keep
It a secret anymore.
Talk about love, honesty and friendship
from your neighbors.

HOW DO WE LEARN OR TEACH
LECTURE
VISUAL
PROPS
AUDIO
HANDS ON
GROUP DISCUSSIONS
LITERATURE
BRAIN STORMING
BUZZ GROUPS
PROMPTING QUESTIONS
ANSWERING QUESTIONS

SELF STUDY
MENTORING – MASTER TAUGHT
ROLE PLAYING
FROM EACH OTHER
TESTING
FROM EXPERIENCE
OBSERVING

WHAT CAN WE LEARN
KNOWLEDGE
SKILL
WISDOM
TO BE A BETTER PERSON

HOW DO WE GET THERE
DETERMINATION
PERSISTENCE
ATTITUDE

HATS OFF TO THE LADY TRUCKER

In our book we talk about him most of the time.
So ladies when you read this book, where it says
him, you say her – I hope that's fair with you.
I know lady truckers get a lot of flack out there,
as my wife is a lady trucker also.
Over the years during our travels, we came across
a few immature truckers who feel women should
be at home in the kitchen – that the highway is no place for a
woman and they are new to the industry.

A friend of mine says he knows some male truckers
that would be better off in the kitchen.
The lady driver is not new to the industry.
I know women truckers who have been driving
for many years.
<small>A few examples:</small>
Back in the early 1960's there was a lady trucker
that hauled mobile homes from Washington to
Alaska for many years. I traveled the Alaska Highway at that time,
and not once did
I see her in a predicament.

Another lady that drove our highways was
Gloria, the first lady trucker to travel the Dempster Highway from
Whitehorse Yukon to Inuvik North
west Territories, She was also an excellent trucker.

Once our family were grown, my wife started
traveling and driving with me. She has driven the
highways just mentioned, along with Vancouver to
Toronto Canada. She has driven all the US states
with the exception of four, accident free –
a plug for myself (she had a good instructor).

Lady truckers are out there and most of them
are doing a great job.

So I have to say this to Mr trucker –
rather than ridicule and verbal abuse, why don't
you see if you can be of any help to all truckers.

It's called **"teamwork"**.

HOW TO DEAL WITH STRESS

When you're stressed out your body releases chemicals in response to stress without sufficient time to recover. This can wear the body down, and causes many symptoms headaches and muscle tension, high blood pressure, chest pain, tiredness, sleeping problems, indigestion, changes in appetite, anger, and edginess, anxiety, nervousness, depression, clouded thinking, substance abuse, which can lead to illness.
It is estimated that 75 – 90% of all visits to the doctor are stress related.

Stress also relates to some of the top killers;
Heart disease, cancer, lung cancer and so on.

To help relieve stress, Here are a few ideas:

Change what you can and release what you can't.
Keep your attitude positive.
Surround yourself with positive people.
Relax your mind and body when possible.
Some ways to relax are:
Stretching, deep breathing, meditation, and thinking good things.
If your stress limit is too high and you are having trouble with day to day activities – Then get help.
There is no shame in asking for help, it will make you a better person.
Life is a growing experience.

HOURS OF SERVICE

Due to the ever changing and differences
Between Canada and the United States
Hours of service rules, we want to make
you aware of the importance of checking
both jurisdictions current regulations.

Be aware of the extensive fines and
penalties of which you are liable for.

Source information available:

1. Dispatcher
2. Local Authorities
3. Internet information
Remember – **The Onus is on you**

HOURS OF SERVICE – U.S.A.

Know and understand the workings of the log book
If unsure ask for help and some good training or advice, this will
save you many dollars in fines,
not knowing is no excuse.
Here is how the hours of service work in the U.S.A.

You are allowed to drive up to 11 hours in a 14 hour period – after
a 10 hour break.
This break must be 8 hours in the sleeper with 2 hours off duty to
equal 10 hours off duty.
The system works this way:

You can drive for 11 hours and work for 3 hours
for the total of 14 hours per day,
with not more than 70 hours in a 7 day period.
If you work 3 hours and drive 11 hours for 5 days
you total 70 hours.
After taking off 34 hours straight,
the clock restarts at zero.

HOURS OF SERVICE – CANADA

The hours of service are the same as the U.S.A.
except with no restart after 34 hours off duty.
You may drive 13 hours per day with 1 hour work time – not to exceed 70 hours in 7 days.
The 10 hour off rule is not the same as the U.S.A.
It goes like this – 8 consecutive hours in the sleeper
and the 2 hours can be broken into ½ hour segments throughout the day.

Also there is a 14 day rule
plus a north of the 60th parallel rule
and a 2 hour exception rule for bad weather,
roads, or unforeseen delays, only if
you could have completed in normal time
of less than 2 hours allowed.

If you don't know or completely understand the log book or hours of service – Ask for training.
A true professional asks questions and takes proper training, that's how you become a true team player.

IMPORTANT MESSAGES

Fire

Have you practiced fire drills at home? If you have a two storey house – Have a rope ladder readily accessible to escape a fire from the top floor.

If you are in a flash flood area – talk about and explain what procedures to use for safety.

A few examples are:

Never try to walk or drive through a flooded area.
Move to higher ground.
Follow evacuation advice and take routes recommended immediately.
Remember – There are no shortcuts.

Earthquakes

If you are a home or in a building, take cover and stay put. Protect your head and body under a desk or table. Stay calm and ask others to do likewise.

After an earthquake – check for gas leaks, electrical problems, and any structural damage.
Just to mention a few things

If you are in a vehicle stay away from bridges and overpasses – Move to higher ground.

Some other items and things you should become
Aware of and make yourself familiar with are:

Bomb threats
Suspicious mail
Wild fires
Terrorism indicators

Try to prepare yourself and your family,
to be ready for any disasters.

An ounce of prevention
Is worth a ton of wisdom.

To get more information
on the above mentioned practices and drills
Contact: The Red Cross
Go on the internet
The Library
Your local telephone directory

Remember – Practice makes Perfect.

IDLING TIME AND FUEL COSTS

At anytime of the year your truck must **not** be left idling, during meal breaks, coffee shops, loading and unloading, etc.
Speed and idling time are the major contributors
to high fuel consumption.

An idling truck can use 5 to 10 liters of fuel per hour, idling a diesel engine for more than 3 minutes may clog injectors, making an engine less powerful and less efficient.
When idling the engine set at 1000 rpm and in extreme weather set at approximately 1500 rpm.

JOKES

This has to one of the most effective
ads ever printed.
"SINGLE BLACK FEMALE" seeks male companionship
ethnicity unimportant.
I'm a very good looking girl who LOVES to play. I love long walks in the woods, riding in your pickup, hunting ,camping, fishing trips, cozy winter nights lying by the fire. Candlelight dinners will have me eating out of your hand. I'll be at the front door when you get home from work wearing
only what nature gave me.
Call(###) ###-#### and ask for Daisy,
I'll be waiting.
Over 15,000 men found themselves talking to the local humane society about an 8-week-old
Black Labrador retriever.

A couple of old guys were golfing when one said he was going to get a new set of dentures. His friend remarked that he had gone to the same dentist for dentures a few years before.
"Oh?" the first said "Did he do a good job?"

"Well I was on the course yesterday when a fellow hooked a shot, he said.
The ball must have been going 200 mph when it hit me right between the legs."
"What does that have to do with your teeth? Asked the first.
"Well he explained, "that was the first time in two years that my teeth didn't hurt.

A MAN GOES TO VISIT HIS 85 YEAR OLD GRANDPA IN THE HOSPITAL

"How are you Grandpa?" he asks,
"Feeling fine, says the old man.
"What's the food like?" Terrific, wonderful menus"
"And the nursing?" "Just couldn't be better.
These young nurses really take care of you."
"What about sleeping? Do you sleep ok?
"No problem nine hours solid every night.
At 10 o'clock they bring me a cup of hot chocolate and a Viagra tablet …and that's it. I go out like,"
The grandson is puzzled and a little alarmed by this, so he rushes off to question the nurse in charge.
"What are you people doing?" he says, I'm told
You're giving an eighty year old man Viagra on a daily basis. Surely that can't be true?" "Oh yes replies the nurse. Every night we give him a cup of hot chocolate and a Viagra tablet. It works wonderfully well.
The chocolate makes him sleep,---

And the Viagra stops him from rolling out of bed.

Old Digger

THE THINKER

An elderly man in Louisiana had owned a
large farm for several years.
He had a large pond in the back.
It was properly shaped for swimming, so he
fixed it up nice – picnic tables, horseshoe courts,
and some apple and peach trees.
One evening the old farmer decided
to go down to the pond and check it out, as he
hadn't been there for a while, and look it over.
As he neared the pond, he heard voices shouting
and laughing with glee. As he came closer
he saw it was a bunch of young women
skinny-dipping in his pond.
He made the women aware of his presence
and they all went to the deep end.
One of them shouted to him, "We're not
coming out until you leave!"
The old man frowned, " I didn't come down
here to watch you ladies swim naked,
or to make you get out of the pond."
Holding the bucket up he said,
"I'm here to feed the alligator."
Moral of the story;

Some old men can still think fast.

LOAD SECUREMENT

You must know how to secure a load and be able to explain why and how it is secure.
When a load is secured properly, it must withstand all maneuvers your truck will make in an emergency, quick stop or turn.
Tiered articles the first 6 feet must be tied
separate from the top load.
When hauling pipe – Remember
the Oilfield Belly Wrap.
If you're not sure – Ask someone.

LENGTH
Tie down guide for number of tie downs is:
2 tie downs for the first 2.5 meters and 1 tie down
for every 2.5 meters thereafter.

WEIGHT
A load weighing 15,000 lbs. needs 3 tie downs
if the working load is 5,000 lbs or better.
Example: If tie downs load limit is 3,000 lbs,
and the load limit is 15,000 lbs
you would need 5 tie downs.

SOME LOAD SECUREMENT PROBLEMS

Insufficient numbers of tie downs.
Loose debris and blocking material.
Slack tie downs – Outside of the rub rail
Tie downs hooked to the rub rail.
Damaged tie downs.

Bungee cords can only be used on tarps
not for load securement.

If unsure of the proper tie downs,
ask the questions – Be safe - Not Sorry

Remember more tie downs may be
required to secure the load safely.

The sum of the working load limits – from all tie downs must be
at least 50% of the weight
of the cargo.

Be aware of unsafe tie downs that have got into our marketing system. Make sure the tie downs you use are marked or stamped with a weight of strength on them, as this is how inspectors grade your load
safe or unsafe.

Remember – you are responsible for the safety of your load, so make double sure your load is safe.

If you have any doubt – add another belt or chain,
this is cheap insurance.

Do not use frayed or inferior products.
It is your responsibility to make sure all tie downs you use – meet the National Safety Code.

LIGHTS

THE HIGHWAY TRAFFIC ACT
RULES AND REGULATIONS FOR LIGHTS

Low Beam – Should be aimed so that lights will reveal persons or vehicles at a distance of at least 30 meters.

High Beam – Should be aimed so that lights will reveal persons or vehicles at a distance of at least 100 meters.

Tail Lamps – Shall be red and visible of not less than 150 meters.

Stop lights – Must be visible for a distance of no less than 250 meters.

NEVER OVERDRIVE YOUR LIGHTS

LAW ENFORCEMENT

Treat law enforcement officers with respect

and how you would like to be treated.

Without enforcement on Safety

Rules and Regulations,

our highways would not be safe.

Not to mention how unsafe

our equipment would be.

Industry and bad drivers have brought

on most of the reasons – for these

rules and regulations.

The good work of drivers abiding by the

rules and the enforcement officers overseeing this,

makes and keeps our highways

a safer place to be.

MEETING

A good meeting or get together is like
sharpening the saw (so to say.)
Today we want input from you –
How do we make it better –
by sharing information.
Seek first to understand,
then be understood.
Don't be too quick to diagnose
without giving some thought.

MEAL ALLOWANCE

Too many truckers, bus drivers, and business
travelers are missing out on a reasonable meal allowance by
neglecting to take advantage of regulations within the Income Tax Act
that allow them to take the civil servant rate
for their meals and incidentals,
income tax free each year.
There is a form to fill out for your meals,
we recommend you discuss this with your accountant.

MONEY

It's not how much you make
Rather – How you spend it.
So save all your receipts and
claim as much as you can at Tax Time.

METRIC CONVERSION TIPS

Kilometers to miles
1 Mile = 1.609 Kilometers
1 Kilometer = .621 Miles

Approximate miles to kilometers per hour

110 kilometers per hour = 70 miles per hour
100 kilometers per hour = 60 miles per hour
80 kilometers per hour = 50 miles per hour
50 kilometers per hour = 30 miles per hour

Weight
1 kilogram = 2.2046 pounds
1 pound = .454 kilograms

Length
1 foot = .3048 meters
1 meter = 3.282 feet

Liters to Gallons
1 liter = .264 gallons
1 gallon = 3,785 liters

Temperature
32 degrees Fahrenheit = 0 degrees Celsius
That is the freezing point

212 degrees Fahrenheit = 100 degrees Celsius
That is the boiling point

NORMAL COMMERCIAL DRIVER

Is kind and considerate
Follows posted speeds in ideal conditions
He drives according to traffic
and weather conditions

Examples:

Not blocking passing lanes
Slowing down for night travel
Not switching from lane to lane
Not tailgating
He has a positive attitude
Taps his brakes to advise slowing down
Uses signal lights appropriately
Doesn't flash headlights
Doesn't turn in front of oncoming traffic
Doesn't abuse the CB
Abides by the rules and regulations of our industry
He and his equipment meet the NSC code
Doesn't get involved with aggressive drivers
Takes rests when required
Looks fresh, joking and happy at the end of the trip
Turns negatives into positives
A True Team Player
Making a better name for our industry.

NOTES

PERSONAL PRINCIPLES

1. Always be active.
2. Make few promises.
3. Always speak the truth.
4. Live within your income.
5. Never speak evil of anyone.
6. Keep good company – or none.
7. Live up to your engagements.
8. Never play games of chance.
9. Drink no intoxicating drinks – then drive.
10. Good character is above everything else.
11. Keep your own secrets if you have any.
12. Never borrow if you can possibly avoid it.
13. Marry only when you are able to support a wife.
14. When you speak, look into their eyes.
15. Save when you're young – spend when old.
16. Don't go into debt – if there's a way out.
17. Good company and conversation is a virtue.
18. Your character can be damaged – only by you.
19. Retiring after the day – Did I do well?
20. Am I a good Samaritan?
21. How can I grow more positive?

PROPER ATTITUDES AND SKILLS

1. Be a superb listener.
2. Establish a good attendance record at work , be on time and don't take unnecessary sick days.
3. Maintain a healthy balance between your home and work life so neither suffers.
4. Demonstrate self-motivation.
5. Communicate cheerfully and thoroughly with co-workers, supervisors, and customers.
6. Share only positive information of your workplace.
7. Communicate only reliable information to others.
8. Separate your family and personal relationships.
9. Focus on the positive aspects of your job and try to improve on the negative.
10. Do not make negative comments about co-workers and supervisors, when they are not present.
11. When resigning from a job, do it in a positive manner. Train your replacement so that the productivity does not suffer.
12. Don't step on other people while climbing the success ladder. Make sure that others will be happy when you succeed.
13. If you train and teach people the right way and help them become the very best, when you advance or move on to another job – they can take over your position without loss of production.
And you have done a good job.

PERSISTENCE

Persistence is the ability to overcome obstacles along the way.

PERSONALITY TRAITS

1. Establish and maintain a strong relationship with your supervisor without alienating your co-workers.

2. Be a good producer yourself and contribute to the productivity of your co-workers and supervisor.

3. Maintain a positive attitude under a difficult supervisor until changes occur (this can sometimes be very challenging; but persevere.)

4. Establish mutually rewarding relationships with co-workers who are not as productive as you.

5. Maintain your productivity without alienating co-workers who are not as productive as you.

6. Avoid extreme highs or lows in your productivity regardless of new or difficult changes in your work environment.

7. Report your mistakes or misjudgments, do not try to hide them.

8. Turn any change or challenge into an opportunity.

9. Accept a new supervisor even if he/she has a different leadership style.

10. Do not turn small gripes into major upsets.

11. Send out positive verbal and non verbal signals in all your dealings with others. (in person, on the telephone, in memos etc.)

12. Remain positive if you must work with people who are negative or insensitive.

13. Deal with everyone in an honest and moral way.

14. Avoid racial or sexual remarks.

15. Maintain a sense of humor, especially when things are not going your way.

16. If you begin to become negative, recognize and improve you attitude immediately.

BUILDING AND MAINTAINING A
GOOD WORK RELATIONSHIP

1. Build and maintain effective working relationships with everyone in your company.
2. Build productive, non-conflictive relationships with those whose values and points of view differ from your own.
3. Build relationships based on mutual respect and reward.
4. Maintain healthy, productive working relationships with everyone, even those who irritate you.
5. Treat everyone, regardless of their race or position in the company, with respect.
6. Work efficiently with others, no matter what their sexual orientation is.
7. Do not take slights or insults from others personally.
8. Repair injured relationships with co-workers, supervisors, and customers quickly. Do not let a bad situation fester and get worse. Even if you are not responsible for the damage to a working relationship, take the initiative to restore it. Doing so will protect your career and cause you a lot less stress.
9. Allow others to restore injured relationships with you. It is unproductive and stressful to nurture a grudge.
10. Try not to become upset with people on the job. Release your anger in a proper manner.
11. Take a break or go for a walk. Ask yourself –

How is the best way to handle this? How would the other person handle this situation?

PATIENCE IS A VIRTUE

All it takes is one person with an improper attitude and lack of patience to make things go wrong.
A road and of itself is never unsafe, regardless of weather conditions. It is the drivers on the road that make it unsafe. Our driving attitude is what determines our driving record and how safe we drive down the road. The trucking industry's enviable safety record is not a result of a jury's inquest, better enforcement or more harassment by the law, but it is a result of trucking companies and their employees continually striving to do a safe job with an abundance of patience.
When driving, I encourage all drivers to be very patient with your fellow motorists.

PRAISE FOR DRIVERS ABIDING BY THE RULES

There are a lot of truckers out there that abide by the rules and drive like true professionals. They are kind, courteous and friendly.

These guys are relaxed, very calm and never
seem to be in too big of a hurry.
They always deliver on time, with very
few problems with the load or equipment.

PAPERWORK

What to Toss and What to Keep

As operating costs continue to rise more and more
truckers are beginning to realize that in order to survive they need
to start becoming businessmen first and truckers second.

The key ingredient to becoming a businessman is
learning how to track your income and your expenses so you can
take advantage of all the tax breaks you're entitled to and you'll
know whether you're making a profit or not.
Not at the end of the month, but
from day to day.

Probably the single most common problem for truckers is keeping
a set of books. Years of bad habits telling them to just throw that
receipt in the trash, or file it away in a box to give to the accountant
at the end of the year.
Lost receipts mean lost deductions – deductions that
may mean the difference between just getting by

and making a profit. You need to not only keep those receipts you need to keep them organized.

You need to set up some kind of accounting system to keep track of your expenses.

So how do you get started?

The first thing to understand is what records to keep.

Anything that you spend in or around your truck is a business expense. Whether you're a company driver or an owner operator the gloves you buy for fueling are tax deductible, but only if you have a record of the purchase and a receipt to back it up. Other common items include antennas, batteries (for the flashlight, as well as the truck), binders, blankets, boots, briefcase, calculator, CB repairs, CBs, cellular phones, chains, checking account fees etc.

It is also very important to keep track of all your meals and lodging receipts.

Check with your accountant to see what you should be filing and turning in at the end of the year.

PHONETIC ALPHBET

You may, when reporting an emergency by telephone, be requested to use the phonetic alphabet to spell the complete name of the material in question, to ensure accuracy.

It is as follows:

A	Alpha	N	November
B	Bravo	O	Oscar
C	Charlie	P	Papa
D	Delta	Q	Quebec
E	Echo	R	Romeo
F	Foxtrot	S	Sierra
G	Golf	T	Tango
H	Hotel	U	Uniform
I	India	V	Victor
J	Julia	W	Whiskey
K	Kilo	X	X ray
L	Lima	Y	Yankee
M	Mike	Z	Zulu

PLACARDING

1. Placarding of vehicles must be complete in accordance with the appropriate Govt. Regs.
2. All dangerous goods shipments must be placarded when the total combined shipping weight exceeds 500 kgs or 1100 lbs. Exceptions to the above are for shipments of the following classes: When transporting any Class 1, Class 2.3, Class 2.4, Class 4.3, Class 5.2, Class 7, Class 9.3 products, placards are to be applied to the vehicle regardless of quantity shipped, including empty cylinders being returned. Note: the only exception to this regulation is for shipments of Class 1.4. These do not require any placards for shipments under 1,000 kgs or 2,200 lbs. in addition Class 9.2 products do not require placards at any time.

The following placarding examples have been prepared to assist you in fulfilling your obligation.

	Shipment		Placard Required
A.	300 lb. of Class 8	A.	none
B.	300 lb. of Class 8 1,600 lb of Class 3	B.	Danger placards or Class 3, and 4 Class 8, placards
C.	300 lb of Class 8 1,600 lb of Class3 5 lb of Class 4.3	C.	Danger and Class 4.3 or Class 3, Class 8, and Class 4.3
D.	60 lb of Class 7	D.	Class 7
E.	100 lb of Class 8 100 lb of Class 3 50 lb of Class 2.3	E.	Class 2.3 only

Note: The danger placard may be used in place of the appropriate class card placard only when the total combined weight of all shipments in the same trailer exceeds 500 kgs or 1,100 lbs.

When transporting shipment in Class 1,2.3,2.4,4.3,5.2,7,or 9.3 in conjunction with other classes, the Danger placard may be used if (the total of all) classes of Dangerous Goods exceed 500 kgs or 1,100 lbs. provided the appropriate aforementioned placard is applied as well.

Remember, many of the regulations surrounding the proper transport of Dangerous Goods are structured around you, the employee. As such, the company will not be responsible for you should you fail to adhere to the basic regulatory procedures regarding your general responsibilities.

Placarding:
1. Are they visible from all sides of the vehicle. Are subsidiary risk placards required.
2. Does the Product Identification Number (PIN) appear if required.
3. Are replacements available if lost or damaged during transport.

Note: Placards must not be removed until all residues are removed. (cleaned or purged).

PROFESSIONAL DRIVER'S OPINION
ON ONE BAD THING IN OUR INDUSTRY

In answer to the second part of the question, we would have to say that we feel Log Book Audits appear more for the purpose of generating revenue for the department conducting the audits, than for the purpose of ensuring Safety issues for the drivers and the general public. If in fact, these audits were safety orientated, then fines, quite extensive fines, would not be issued for such things as mistakes in addition, perhaps a missed signature on a log sheet, or heaven forbid it was not really Thursday the seventh but the eighth. A forgotten postal code on the second portion of the daily log, can hardly be considered a safety issue. Not only are the drivers liable for the fines levied, but the company employing the drivers also need to pay double the amount. This procedure should be designated to the same destiny as the Gun Registry program, but hopes of seeing that are slim to none.

In this industry you just have to remember –

The cup is ½ full –too bad it's sour milk though.

Just our opinion

Alan & Judy

PROFESSIONAL DRIVER'S OPINION ON ONE GOOD THING IN OUR INDUSTRY

We have considered and prepared the following article to address the question – to list something that we feel is good within the trucking industry, and should be retained, and also something we feel is not good and should be changed.

Therefore, in our opinion, we would list the Safety Inspections as something we feel is a very good thing. As the operator of a vehicle which travels most often on a daily basis, one would have to agree that they would be most confident knowing that the vehicle of which they are operating must be in top mechanical condition. For your own safety, first of all but perhaps more important you can be confident that the safety of others is not jeopardized by a vehicle that is not in 100% condition.

Another benefit to be realized is that, by making sure your vehicle is capable of passing inspections at any given time, requires constant attention.

By keeping on top of your vehicles mechanical condition equates to good preventative maintenance
practices which is proven to save money, which goes back in the owners pocket.

Care and attention paid to the vehicle you are operating, being sure that is it is in the best mechanical condition it can be is merely a reflection of a truly Professional Driver. To pass safety inspections, is really a compliment to the driver.

PROTECTING YOURSELF
FROM IDENTITY THEFT

This is one of the fastest growing crimes in America today. Don't think this can't happen to you.
Approximately 3 out of every 100 people have their identity stolen. Contact your local government for advice on how to prevent this from happening to you.

One business scam out there is: "We need your checking account number to confirm your credit worthiness."

Be Careful

The next time you order checks have only your initials (instead of your first and last name put on them).

Do not sign the back of your credit cards. Instead put photo ID required.

When you are writing checks to pay on your credit card accounts, **Do Not** put the complete number on the "for" line. Instead, just put the last four numbers,

The credit card company knows the rest of the number, and anyone who might be handling your check as it passes through all the check processing channels won't have access to it.

Put your work phone on your checks instead of your home phone. If you have a PO Box use that instead of your home address. If you do not have a PO Box, use your work address. Never have your SS# or SIN# printed on your checks. (DUH!) You can add it if necessary. But if you have it printed, anyone can get it.

Place the contents of your wallet on a photo copy machine. Do both sides of each license, credit card etc. etc. You will know what you had in your wallet and all the account numbers and phone numbers to call and cancel. Keep the photocopy in a safe place.

STOLEN CARDS

We have been told we should cancel our credit cards immediately. But the key is having the toll free numbers and your card numbers handy so you know whom to call. Keep these where you can find them.
File a police report immediately in the jurisdiction where the credit cards etc. were stolen.

Call the 3 national organizations immediately to place a fraud alert on your name and SS#
The alert means any company that checks your credit knows the information was stolen, and they have to contact you by phone to authorize credit.
Social Security Administration: 1-800-269-0271

WHO DO YOU CONTACT

Here are the numbers you always need to contact if your wallet, cards etc., have been stolen.
Equifax: 1-800-535-6285
Experian (formerly TRW): 1-888-397-3742
Trans Union: 1-800-680-7289
Social Security Admin (fraud) 1-800-269-0271

TIRED OF GETTING CREDIT CARD OFFERS?

Credit card companies gain access to information contained in your credit report without your knowledge or consent. Each time your credit report is accessed your credit score is lowered. You have the right to prohibit information contained in your file maintained by the credit reporting agencies from being used in a credit transaction not initiated by you by calling 1-888-567-8688 or by writing:

TRANSUNION LLC, Att: Marketing Opt-Out, PO Box 97328, Jackson, MS 39288 – 7328
EQUIFAX, Information Service Center, PO Box 1055873, Atlanta, GA 30348
EXPERIAN, PO Box 2104 Allen TX 75013-2104
Always be defensive of your identity and financial information

KEY CARDS

Although key cards differ from hotel to hotel and motel to motel, there could be a problem of theft out there.
Theft prevention has discovered the following:

These key cards contain:

1. The customers name.
2. Customers partial home address.
3. Room number
4. Check in and check out dates
5. Customers credit card number and expiry date

Any dishonest hotel or motel employee that has access to this information, could scan the information and use the same.
The bottom line is –
Dispose of these cards yourself or ask the clerk to clear the card while you watch.

CREDIT CARDS

Half of the states in the USA allow you to freeze your credit. So if someone tries to open a new line of credit in your name, the application is denied.

THERE IS A DOWNSIDE TO THIS

If you are applying for a new credit card or loan, you will have to wait a few days to get approved.

THE GOOD SIDE TO THIS

Means you won't be tempted to apply for more credit cards, and impulse buying.

QUESTION: ASKED TO DRIVERS
WHAT IS THE BEST PIECE OF ADVICE YOU HAVE RECEIVED OR GIVEN REGARDING THE TRUCKING BUSINESS?

Professional driving experience: 17 years

Be patient. You'll learn what it takes, but you aren't going to learn everything all at once.
Don't be pressured by other people. My wife drives to and she is always being pressured into doing something she doesn't feel comfortable doing
"My advice is Just Be Patient".

Professional driving experience: 63 years

Don's advice to anyone behind the wheel is:
The time you think you know it all –
Is the time to quit driving. You're going to hurt yourself or somebody else
"If you think you know it all"

Professional driving experience: 28 years

Never stop trying to make it in this business. You might not succeed at first, but keep at it. Too many new or young drivers, give up too soon. If you work hard and keep at it you will be successful.
"You'll never know if you give up."

Professional driving experience: 38 years

Think real hard and ask yourself - is this what I want to do for the rest of my life?
Are you ready to give up your home life?
"It's either in the blood – or it's not.
People that don't have it in their blood
don't need to be out there."

QUESTION: ASKED TO DRIVERS
IF YOU COULD CHANGE ONE THING ABOUT THE TRUCKING INDUSTRY,
WHAT WOULD IT BE?

Professional driving experience: 13 years

"The attitude of some of the drivers."
There are a lot of guys out here who don't know what they're doing. They're not safety conscious, nor do they care to be given any good advice.
There's no unity amongst the drivers.
There's no camaraderie like there used to be.
When I first started driving, the older drivers were very helpful to the new guys. Now everyone is for themselves. That's a shame, as it doesn't have to be that way.

Professional driving experience: 11 years

It's tough enough being a woman in this business, and some of these drivers make it even harder.
You try to keep your radio on channel 19
to get information, but ever time you open your mouth, you get verbally assaulted.
A lot of the guys out there are nice.
Then you have those who are
down right rude.
They hide behind the radio because they're not man enough to say it to your face.
"If I could change anything, I would so something about the foul mouthed idiots."

Professional driving experience: 28 years

I suppose if I could change one thing,
it would have to be the pay scale.
I think drivers should get more money
for what we do.

Professional driving experience: 11 years

"I would change the attitude of some drivers." Too many people have had bad attitudes, and that gives the rest of us a bad rap. Listen to channel 19 on the CB, you'll know what I'm talking about…*very unprofessional.*

ROAD RAGE

Road Rage is increasing all the time.
Many people are getting hurt unnecessarily,
and this must be stopped.

When you become involved in road rage,
you have played into the other person's hand.
" He wins – You Lose"

So stay positive and be the *True Professional*

ROAD RAGE – IS SUCH A SENSELESS ACT

THE RIGHT TO REFUSE

If your equipment, the load, or yourself
do not meet the National Safety Code.

Example:
You do not have the proper equipment
for that particular load, you cannot secure
the load properly.

You do not have enough knowledge or
experience to haul that particular load.

You have the right to refuse to leave
with that particular load.

SMILE

A smile costs nothing, but gives so much.
It enriches those who receive,
without making poorer those who give.
It takes but a moment,
but the memory of it lasts forever.
None is so rich or mighty that he
can get along without it.
A smile creates happiness in the home,
fosters good will in business,
and is the countersign of friendship.
It brings rest to the weary,
Cheer to the discouraged,
Sunshine to the sad,
and is nature's best antidote for trouble.

It can't be bought, begged, borrowed or stolen,
for it is something of **NO VALUE**
until it is **GIVEN AWAY.**

Some people are too tired to give you a smile.
Give them one of yours.

As no one needs to smile so much,
as he who has none to give.

Some Needed Books

National Safety Code (Canada)

Federal Motor Carrier Safety Regulations (USA)

TDG (Canada - Hazmat (USA)

Load Securement (BC) Canada

Emergency Handbook –
What to do when seconds count

Work safely behind the wheel. –
Workers Compensation – AB

SOME COURSES OR EXAMS THAT WE SHOULD HAVE AND MANEUVERS WE SHOULD KNOW
First Aid

Heimlich Maneuver

Fire Safety

Proper Lifting

Proper Eating Habits

Three Point Entrance and Exit

SOME DRIVING DISTRACTIONS

Route Problems

In Vehicle Distractions

Scenery

Accidents

The Other Driver

SOME EXAMPLES OF BEING A "SEEING EXPERT"

Get The Big Picture

Leave Yourself an "Out"

Make Sure You Are Seen

Keep Your Eyes Moving

SIX SECRETS OF HIGH ENERGY PEOPLE

DO SOMETHING NEW

RECLAIM LIFE'S MEANING

PUT YOURSELF IN THE FUN ZONE

BID FAREWELL TO GUILT AND REGRET

DECIDE TO BETTER YOURSELF

THE MORE YOU GIVE
THE MORE YOU RECEIVE

SUCCESS IS A CHOICE – NOT LUCK

SAFE WORK PRACTICES
Entering and Exiting
Always use 3 point entrance and exit
procedures on or around vehicles.
This maneuver will prevent most accidents
or injuries, entering and exiting equipment.

Be involved in safety as much as you can.
Share your thoughts and ideas.
If unsure – **Ask the Questions**
Know your responsibilities

SAFETY TIP

Slow has four letters – So does life
Speed has five letters – So does death

SLOW VEHICLES

The first thing when catching up to a slow vehicle is
Ask yourself "Why is it going so slow?"
A few reasons:

How are the road conditions?
Are they icy or slippery?
Is he turning?
Is there an accident ahead?
Is the driver looking for a place to pull over?
On hills going up and down,
in some states it is compulsory
that truckers use their 4 way flashers for
Slow moving trucks.

It is your responsibility to know this -
also which states.

SPEEDING HURRY UP DRIVER

These drivers seem to be very unhappy,
complaining about most things,
and the bad day they are having.
My advise to the Hurry Up driver is
Slow down, Smell the Roses,
and have a happier life.

SOME SAFE WORK PRACTICES AND IDEAS

Follow all company safe policy procedures.
Set an example by practicing safety.
Share information of unsafe procedures.
Report and encourage fellow workers
to follow safety rules.
Recognize workers following safe
policies and procedures.
Know the importance of sharing
thoughts and ideas.
Find out if the company has a Discipline and Safety committee in place and who they are.
They should be your (back up team.)
Report any near misses, incidents, or accidents.
Why do we share information on incidents and near misses? – To have fellow workers on the lookout (hopefully not repeating), and eliminating the grey areas.
Know and understand Due Diligence
and it's importance.
Do proper Pre and Post trips.

SAFETY TIP – THINK BEFORE YOU LIFT

Keep what you are lifting close to your body.
Lift with your legs – Not your back
Use your feet to turn – Not your back
Be a true team player.
Share your thoughts and ideas,
to improve operations.
If unsure – ask questions
All wise people ask questions.

SAFETY GEAR

Safety boots, safety glasses, safety vest, gloves, hard hat, fire retardant coveralls (if required.)

If hauling Dangerous Goods
have a spill kit.

Always wear a safety vest when getting out of your vehicle – along or beside it.

Approximately 63% of all drivers killed on our highways, were out of their vehicle.

Never wear nylon, polyester or synthetic clothing under fire retardant clothing, as these will stick to your skin

SAFE WORK HAZARDS

Before starting work ask yourself the following questions and identify the hazards – and think.

1. Could any part of the body get caught in or between objects?

2. Do tools, machines, or equipment present any hazards?

3. Can the worker be harmed if there is contact with the machine?

4. Can the worker slip, trip, or fall?

5. Can the worker suffer strain from lifting, pushing, or pulling?

6. Is the worker exposed to extreme heat or cold?

7. Is there a danger from falling objects?

8. Is lighting a problem?

9. Can weather conditions affect safety?

10. Is harmful radiation a problem?

11. Can contact be made with hot, toxic, or caustic substances?

12. Are there fumes, vapors, dusts, or mists in the air?

13. Wear a mask when sweeping out a van.

14. If unsafe or unsure – don't proceed.

SPILL CLEANUP
SUGGESTED PROCEDURES

1. Clear the area, and notify the appropriate authorities.
2. Determine the nature of the spill. From a safe location, obtain and deploy appropriate personal protective equipment.
3. Approach the spill with caution. Deploy sorbent socks around the spill to prevent its spread. Never step into the spill.
4. When the spill is contained, move sorbent socks on the ground toward the center of the spill. When containment socks begin to reach their saturation points, add more sorbents directly to the spill and continue to advance toward the center.
5. In the event that the spill is larger than the available sorbent capacity, socks and sheets can be wrung out in an appropriate container and reused with the same chemical.
6. When the spill has been absorbed, place all used sorbents into the disposable bags. Store in a safe location until proper disposal can be arranged.
7. Immediately restock used equipment to be prepared for another spill.

SPEEEDING AND THE AGGRESSIVE DRIVER

Speeding and aggressive driving is the number one cause of accidents and death in
North America - increasing by 68% per year.
The aggressive driver is not aware of his actions or doesn't care. If he only knew some of the
statistics; he may slow down and not be a road warrior, realizing that he only shares our
highways and that he doesn't own them.
He gives our industry a bad reputation.
A few examples of his style:

Tailgating – a very unsafe procedure
Headlight flashing – Cutting off other vehicles
Deliberately blocking off other vehicles – Verbal abuse – assault on a vehicle or person –
Obscene gestures – improper signals or none at all.
The speeding, inconsiderate driver doesn't realize that his bad driving habits is creating his own stress, anger, and fatigue. Does he know
that the posted speed limits are for ideal conditions. The faster driver may save 30
minutes in a 1000 mile run, pass over 2000 vehicles, be passed by 10 – 15 vehicles, use his brakes 12 – 14 hundred times, and still be late for his load or offload appointment. He also reduces his ability to avoid an accident and increases the probability of death or injury

(to mention a few).

He looks played out and unhappy at the end of
his trip. Turning what should have been
a positive – into a negative.

SUBSTANCE ABUSE POLICY

The possession of and or consumption of alcohol,
illegal drugs, or the misuse of prescriptions drugs is strictly
prohibited on company property, in company vehicles, as well as
in circumstances deemed to present a serious risk to the concerns
of the company, as to the client and employee safety, it's financial
integrity, security and safety of its property as well as public
reputation.
Any employee taking a legal drug or medication
whether or not prescribed by a doctor, which is
known to possible effect or impair judgment,
coordination or perception so to adversely affect the
ability to perform work must notify his
employer or supervisor.
All employees are expected to perform to the standards set forth
in their respective job descriptions. Declines in work performance
due to substance abuse will be addressed initially in the same
manner as performance deterioration for any other reasons.
However, the use of alcohol or illegal drugs on company property,
in company vehicles, or while on duty is grounds for
immediate dismissal.

SIX POSITIONS OF
THE TWO VEHICLE ACCIDENT

The vehicle ahead
The vehicle behind
Meeting a vehicle
Vehicle at intersection
You overtake and pass
The passing vehicle

A preventable collision is one in which you failed to do everything to prevent it.

Statistics say that 63% of all truck drivers killed – are out of their vehicles checking the equipment or load.

Learn all you can about Safety and Defense – to eliminate as much as possible.

Rear end collisions are mainly multi-vehicles involved – due to tailgating on bad roads or poor visibility.

Remember: Speed limits are posted for ideal conditions. When are conditions ideal?
When there is not a cloud in the sky.
Or on a straight road with no one on it.

SLOW has four letters in it – so does **LIFE**
SPEED has five letters – so does **DEATH**

SOME STATISTICS ON FATAL COLLISIONS

Two vehicle	40%
Off road	25%
Pedestrians	15%
Motorcycle	11%
Miscellaneous	3%
Fixed Object	2%
Rail Road Crossing	1%

While driving- it is very important that you
stay alert and watch out for:
construction workers, wildlife, speeding
drivers under the influence,
vehicles passing on your right, emergency
vehicles, (be prepared to move over and stop.)

HAVE A SAFE DRIVE

SELF ASSESSMENT QUIZ

1. You are traveling 100 kms / hr on dry pavement, when you see a collision blocking the road 70 meters ahead. If you apply the brakes immediately, will your vehicle stop before you hit the vehicle?
   YES   No
2. From the above question if your answer is no, how fast would you be traveling?
   5 – 16 – 32 – 44 – 60 kms /hr
3. Your drivers seat should be adjusted so your hips are higher than your knees.
   TRUE   FALSE
4. Speeding and aggressive driving is the biggest killer on our highways.
   TRUE   FALSE
5. Cutting people off, driving slowly in the passing lane or tailgating can prompt a negative response.
   TRUE   FALSE

QUIZ ANSWERS

1. NO
2. 44
3. FALSE
4. TRUE
5. TRUE

THE ABSENTEE PARENT

There was this away from home parent. When he was home he had a Honey do list and paid a lot of attention to his wife. Their kids were being very bad at times when he was home. The wife said that she didn't have this problem with them when he was away. So they decided to sit the family down and have a discussion. Out of this discussion, they realized that the kids were being bad to get their dads attention.

Whether good or bad – something I learned that worked well for our family. We had a family discussion night once a week. ie: Every Monday night after our dinner, while still at the dining table, we had an open discussion that we could talk about anything.

A few examples were:

Household chores and duties changed each week.
Is there anything or anyone bugging you?
How's things at school?
Sports activities – how are they going for you?
What to wear and what not to wear.
The list goes on.

THE LADY BEHIND THE MAN BEHIND THE WHEEL

Let's not forget the truckers wife.

- This takes a very special person -
For those of you who don't know her job and lifestyle, it goes like this:

While her man is out on the road – aside from being lonely, she keeps the household together, many of which have a family to raise. She becomes the sole chef, dishwasher, handyman, chauffer, organizer, secretary, and accountant, just to name a few.

YOU GALS ARE INCREDIBLE

TRUCK RIDE

The difference of sliding your fifth wheel one or two notches back or forth, can make a big difference in the quality of your ride.
Not to mention the beating your truck takes,
and shaking it apart.
The same goes for the tire pressure on the steering axle. Get the recommended tire pressure from your tire dealer as to how much air you should have in the tires for the weight you are carrying on that axle.

TEN DIFFERENCES BETWEEN A WINNER AND A LOSER

1. A winner makes mistakes, and says "I was wrong." A loser says: "It wasn't my fault."

2. A winner credits his good luck for winning even though it wasn't good luck. A loser credits his bad luck for losing, but it wasn't bad luck.

3. A winner works harder than a loser and has more time. A loser is always "too busy" staying a failure.

4. A winner goes through a problem, a loser goes around it.

5. A winner shows he's sorry by making up for it. A loser says he's sorry but does the same thing next time.

6. A winner knows what to fight for and what to compromise on. A loser compromises on what he should not and fights for what isn't worth fighting for. Every day is a battle of life and it is very important that we are fighting for the right things – and not wasting time with trivial matter.

7. A winner says "I'm good, but not as good as I ought to be." A loser says: "Well I'm not as bad as a lot of people." A winner looks up to where he is going. A loser looks down at those who've not yet achieved the position he has.

8. A winner respects those who are superior to him and tries to learn from them. A loser resents those who are superior to him and tries to find fault.

9. A winner is responsible for more than his job. A loser says " I only work here."

10. A winner says "There ought to be a better way of doing it." A loser says "Why change it?" "That's the way it's always been done."

**SUCCESS IS A CHOICE – NOT LUCK
DECISIVE PEOPLE RISE TO THE TOP
BECAUSE THEY ARE NOT AFRAID TO
MAKE A DECISION – THEN COMMIT TO IT
OTHERS MAKE EXCUSES –
YOU CANNOT FAIL UNLESS YOU QUIT**

TREAT PEOPLE THE WAY
THEY NEED TO BE TREATED

THE GOLDEN RULE
Do unto others as you would
have them do unto you.

THE PLATINUM RULE
Learn about people as there are four different major
types of people that need to be treated differently.

They are as follows:

1. The Director – Directive
2. The Relater – Supportive
3. The Thinker – Cautious
4. The Socializer – Talkative

Behavioral styles of the Director type of person
1. High ego
2. Strong willed
3. Decisive
4. Effective
5. Desires change
6. Competitive
7. Independent
8. Practical
9. Pushy
10. Important
11. Domineering
12. Attacks first
13. Tough
14. Harsh

Behavioral styles of the Thinking person
1. Perfectionist
2. Sensitive
3. Accurate
4. Persistent
8. Cautious
9. Critical
10. Fears Criticism
11. Slow deciding

5. Serious
6. Needs much info
7. Orderly

12. Judgemental
13. Picky
14. Stuffy

Behavioral styles of the Relater type person

1. Dependable
2. Agreeable
3. Supportive
4. Accepts change slowly
5. Calm
6. Contented
7. Amiable

8. Reserved
9. Insecure
10. Conforming
11. Possessive
12. Awkward
13. Wishy-Washy
14. Unsure

Behavioral styles of the Socializer type person

1. Emotional
2. Enthusiastic
3. Optimistic
4. Persuasive
5. Animated
6. Talkative
7. People orientated

8. Stimulating
9. Disorganized
10. Undisciplined
11. Manipulative
12. Excitable
13. Reactive
14. Vain

This is some information on different types of people. You can be parts of all of the types.

You are the majority of one type, and perhaps a small percentage of the others.

Have some fun with this one

THE TRUCKER AND THE TOURIST

Truckers be aware of the tourist season.
As you know many people out there are driving
RV's in excess of 40 feet, also pulling a car
or utility trailer behind them.
Remember: Most of these people drive a 4 wheel
vehicle for the better part of the year.
Most of the time they are very considerate drivers,
however, from time to time some tend to show
bad timing and judgment.

For example:

Cutting you off
Failing to signal
Driving too fast and swerving
Parking along the side of the road
not leaving room for passing.

Remember: - We truckers travel these roads,
and are familiar with them.
Not so for the first time tourist.

So I say to the trucker, " For a few months of
the year, be kind and considerate to these drivers."
Being rude and inconsiderate,
will not help our industry.

So be the professional – and set a good example.

TEN TIPS FOR SAFE
FUEL - EFFICIENT DRIVING

1. Don't drive aggressively - quick starts, hard stops, and aggressive driving can increase fuel consumption by up to 37%.

2. Drive at the posted speed limit – or less, drive according to road and weather conditions.

3. Don't idle – when you let your vehicle idle longer than 10 seconds, you burn more fuel than you would restarting the engine.

4. Drive only when you need to – leave your vehicle at home whenever possible by walking, biking, carpooling or taking the bus.

5. Plan ahead – If you have to drive, plan the most fuel efficient route in advance.

6. Use your vehicle's air conditioner sparingly – using your air conditioner in stop-and-go traffic can increase fuel consumption by as much as 20%. Open the windows or fresh air vents to cool your vehicle.

7. Measure the inflation level of your tires once a month. A single tire under-inflated by just 8 psi can increase your vehicle's fuel consumption 4%.

8. Use cruise control – on dry, flat wide-open highways to help improve fuel efficiency by maintaining an even speed.

9. Maintain your vehicle properly – a poorly maintained vehicle consumes more fuel, produces higher levels of emissions, requires expensive repairs, and has a low resale value.

10. Safe driving – Is fuel efficient driving.

T.D.G. OR HAZMAT

If you are handling T.D.G. or Hazmat make sure that you are trained and know the importance of handling or transporting dangerous goods.
Make sure that you have a Dangerous Goods certificate from your present place of employment.
The certificate of training is only good for three years, as are most of the certificates in our industry.
Know and understand Shipping Documents
Carry a T.D.G. or Hazmat Driver Handbook with you , also a small spill kit.
You never know when a situation will arise, this way you will be ready,
rather than saying I wish I had one, or nothing will happen to me. (wrong)

TEN COMMON DRIVING MISTAKES

1. Failing to pay attention – "zoning out".

2. Driving while dozy.

3. Becoming distracted in the vehicle radio, cell phone, children, and pets.

4 Failing to adjust to weather conditions.

5. Driving aggressively, tailgating, running red lights, and stop signs etc.

6. Making assumptions about other drivers intentions.

7. Speeding.

8. Changing lanes without checking blind spots and mirrors.

9. Driving while upset.

10. Ignoring essential auto maintenance brakes, lights, etc.

The single biggest contributor to collision is failing to see what is happening.
To be a safe driver you must remain aware of your surroundings at all times.

THE REAL COST OF AN ACCIDENT

1. Compensation and benefits -
   These include charges for medical.
   To rehab lump sum payments as well as survivors payments- to mention a few.

2. Legal expenses – suing and fines
   Example: One company in Ontario was fined $600,000 for three health and safety infractions. Sometimes fines force companies to go out of business.

3. Damage to capital assets.
   Retrieving costs.

4. Lost productivity
   Lost revenue.
   Lost productivity of trained employee

5. Then there is always unforeseen miscellaneous costs.

6. Some costs are incalculable like losing a loved one, a longtime friend or fellow employee.

USE OF SAFETY EQUIPMENT
SAFETY FLARES AND
WARNING TRIANGLES – CANADA

Each unit shall carry certified warning triangles and flares. And drivers must be able to produce them on the demand of a Peace Officer.
If you must have your vehicle stationary on the highway between the time period of sunrise and sunset outside the limits of a city, town or village:
The driver of the vehicle must activate the flashing emergency hazard warning lights and place approved warning devices on the highway in line with the vehicle at a distance of approximately <u>30 meters (100 feet) in front of the vehicle</u> as well as approximately <u>30 meters (100 feet) behind the vehicle.</u>

If you must have your vehicle stationary on the highway between sunset and sunrise or at any time when there in not sufficient light to clearly see persons or vehicles on the highway at a distance of 150 meters (500 feet).

The driver must activate the flashing emergency hazard warning lights and within 10 minutes of becoming stationary place approved warning devices on the highway in line with the vehicle at a distance of approximately <u>75m (250 feet) in front of the vehicle</u> as well as approximately <u>75 meters 250 feet) behind the vehicle.</u>

UTA
THE USED TRUCK ASSOCIATION

**BEFORE PURCHASING A TRUCK
KNOW AND UNDERSTAND
WHY THE USED TRUCK ASSOCIATION
IS SO SUCCESSFUL**

On every state road and super highway and many other ribbons of concrete and asphalt, trucks wind their way crisscrossing our nation. Drivers are at the wheels steering their payloads to every nook and cranny that can be found. These men and, more and more, women need trucks upon which they can depend. They also need accurate information about the largest tool of their trade. Finding a trustworthy source of needed information was often times a challenge.

That is why, back in 1988, a group of individuals got together and called themselves The Used Truck Association. Their mission? To be an impartial organization of used truck professionals and associated businesses who are committed to strengthening the used truck industry. Now numbering over 700 strong and stretched across the nation, their members are dedicated to leading by example in order to improve the reputation of the industry. To that end, they wrote and adopted a tough code of nine ethics by which to operate their

businesses and guide their dealings with each and every customer, including the drivers and owner operators. How does the UTA carry out that mission? Very simply. Through education and training each member in the used truck marketplace learns better ways to operate their businesses, plan ahead for product changes, properly spec trucks, and how to find out from a driver exactly what their rig needs for the routes they will cover. And they will do all this with the highest of standards while promoting the professionalism of the used truck industry as a whole.
The members in good standing of The Used Truck Association subscribe to the following
 UTA Code of Ethics.

Honesty - We represent honestly the products and services they sell and support.

Integrity – We treat all customers, associates, and employees with dignity, respect, and integrity.

Professionalism – We are committed to developing and maintaining, knowledgeable well-trained sales professionals.

Value – We endeavor to provide and represent the best-valued products and services.

Excellence – We are dedicated to excellence in all that we do, all the time.

Continuous Improvement – We constantly re-evaluate our procedures to ensure they are efficient and responsive to customers' needs and wants.

Keeping Promises – We do what we say we are going to do, and we strive to do right the first time.

Complete Satisfaction – Our number one priority is to always provide the best in customer service and satisfaction.

Relationships – We work hard not to make sales, but to build beneficial relations and long-term customers.

Part of our mission is to supply information to the end-users of the equipment we sell.
By going to the website – www.uta.org – you will find several educational publications offering a wealth of information on subjects relevant and useful to you. These publications are easily printed
from a computer. One subject-"What is a Low-Mileage Truck? It's Not What You Might Think"-
fosters an understanding of how mileage as an indicator of a heavy truck's reliability and usefulness has changed. Among the subjects addressed: used truck buyers' perceptions, theory and reality of mileage and used truck worthiness, technological advances of major truck components and their impact on trucks and trucking.

And that's not all. The Used Truck Association
(UTA) has a comprehensive set of guidelines for
"industry standard" trade terms and conditions;
These are used to establish the condition of a used
truck as agreed by both the seller and the buyer.
Are you a candidate for becoming an owner-operator? Then you will want to read our
"Succeeding as an Owner-Operator" publication.
It will give you the insights you need to give it a
proper consideration.

It just makes good sense to do business with good
folks; and members of The Used Truck Association
are good folks. We encourage you to look for, then
shop where you see our blue box logo. You will be
glad you did.

Eddie Walker, President of the UTA

"We cannot say enough about the men and women
who move everything we use in our lives.
Professional drivers are what keep this nation moving. Their unselfishness of spirit, dedication to
their craft, attention to the road, and willingness to
improve are the very qualities that keep a nation strong. "We applaud you all."

From the President of the UTA

WEIGHT LOSS TIP

Walk and lose weight. Walking is by far the best exercise for weight loss. It is also the best exercise you can do for your health. The body is designed to walk. Formalized exercise is not done throughout the world. The majority of people who live to be over 100 years old and have virtually no disease do not do formal exercise. However, they do walk. People throughout the world walk an average of ten miles a day where people from America walk less than a quarter of a mile a day. If you want to lose weight, **walk.** The ideal way to lose weight is by walking for one hour non-stop every day. This is not running, it's not jogging, it's walking. You should be walking at a pace that you feel comfortable with. Some of you will start out very, very slow. Some of you will not even be able to walk a full hour without getting too tired and winded. Start with fifteen minutes and increase to twenty-five minutes, increase that to forty-five minutes, increase it to an hour. It may take you a full month to get to a full hour. It's because people all over the world can walk for hours and hours. People in America can't walk for an hour without getting tired or waking up the next day with sore ankles, knees, hips, and legs. This means that you are in desperate need of walking. If you walk for a full hour and then wake up with any pain, stiffness or discomfort, you are in serious trouble. You are destined for illness and disease.

You are not moving the toxins out of your body, and you are not oxygenating your body, your muscles, tendons, joints, and ligaments are all beginning to deteriorate and you are headed for a disaster. You have to be walking: Walking will reverse your condition and cure you of many ailments. The main thing walking does for weight loss is that it seems to reset your body's set point. Your body has a point that it sets regulating your weight. If you go above this weight, it will regulate back to the set- point weight. If you go below this weight it will regulate it back up to the set- point weight. Your body's set point will determine what your weight is. This is the reason why most people have a certain weight that they stay at. Even if they lose weight, they always bounce back to that weight, or if they gain weight for awhile because of an eating binge, when they start eating normally they kind of revert back to that set-point weight. By walking for one hour everyday for 30 days your body will tend to reset it's set-point If you do this every single day, you will start losing weight automatically and effortlessly. Plus you will feel better, have more energy, sleep better, be less depressed and be happier. When you walk not on a treadmill, but outside, it is important not to stare at the ground while walking but look around you. The process of looking far away at things has a profound effect on your mental state. You won't believe how much better you feel-and you won't believe how easy it is to lose weight without changing anything else.

WHAT IS WISDOM ?

Sharing knowledge

Being a good listener

Having a good attitude

Being wise

Treating people right

Not knowing it all

Knowing your limits

To read other people

What can I learn today

Ask the question

Helping other people

Wisdom consists in knowing what to do with the knowledge one has, and directing that knowledge to the highest and most moral ends.

WINDSHIELDS

Tips for better visibility:
Here's a trick I learned to prevent ice build up
on the wipers and windshield.
Turn the heat off in the cab, and turn the
heat on in the sleeper. I can not explain
how or why it works, but this method
always works for me.

Another tip is to use the windshield treatment
to repel rain, snow and sleet. This also helps and there are many
more remedies in various
truckers magazines.

WINTER SURVIVAL GEAR

Ready to eat meals
Supply of water and drinks
Insulated coveralls
Good warm winter jacket
A few candles and matches
Thermal boots
Insulated mitts
Long johns
Warm socks
Warm hat
Small heater
Blanket
Have these items properly secured

WORK ALONE

Take time to think about safety, your
livelihood, family and friends.

These thoughts will help you
make a cautious and safe decision.

Mixed with a little patience and
a proper attitude also help.

Think twice before doing – if you are
unsure or questioning safety.

DO NOT PROCEED

Take no unnecessary risks.

WATCH THOSE DIESEL PRICES

By going online you can review
the price of diesel at most truck stops.

It pays to shop around and get
the lowest prices.

Every one needs a break
from the rising fuel costs.

YOU HAVE WHAT IT TAKES

You have the wisdom and power to
change within yourself.

Set goals and deadlines for yourself.

Expand your mind to become a better person.

Be kind and considerate to others.

Example:

Help your fellow trucker when he is
backing into a stall at a truck stop,
rather than ridiculing him or her.

Remember when you first started driving,
did you back in perfect on the first try?

Did you consider that maybe that driver
could be having a bad day?

**WHEN YOU'RE KIND AND CONSIDERATE
YOU BECOME A BETTER PERSON
AND FEEL GOOD ABOUT YOURSELF**

NOTES

NOTES